The Weather Door

Martyn Halsall

© Copyright Martyn Halsall 2023

The right of Martyn Halsall to be identified as the author of this work has been asserted in accordance with the Copyright, Designs and Patents Act 1988.

All rights reserved. This book is sold subject to the condition that it shall not, by way of trade or otherwise, be lent, resold, hired out or otherwise circulated without the publisher's prior written consent in any form of cover or binding other than that in which it is published, or in any digital format whatsoever and, in the event of such consent being obtained, only with a similar condition including this condition, being imposed upon the subsequent purchaser.

A CIP catalogue for this book is available from the British Library.

Cover and interior design © copyright Neil Ferber, The Book Mill Press UK

ISBN 978-1-9164750-9-0

The Book Mill Press UK
www.thebookmill.co.uk

For Bella, Emma, Rory, Harry and Grace,
as they navigate the weather forecasts.

About the Author

Martyn Halsall grew up in Lancashire, taught in Dorset and was a student in Chelsea before entering journalism. After working as a reporter on local and regional newspapers he joined *The Guardian* as religious affairs correspondent, later covering industry in the North of England. An award winning poet and journalist, he studied creative writing and creative literary studies at the Universities of Lancaster and Cumbria. He now lives and writes in Northumberland.

Also by Martyn Halsall

Sanctuary (reflecting on a year as the first Poet in Residence at Carlisle Cathedral): Canterbury Press, 2014

Visible Music: Caldew Press, 2020.

Contents

1. Outlook

    Outlook
    Middle Sea View
    The Weather Door
    Weather Maps
    Fieldwork
    Signs
    Closing to Home
    Night Stair

2. Weather Stations

    Chart
    Taking Reference: South East Iceland
    Wearing Viking
    Vote of Thanks: Fair Isle
    Exile: Forties
    Late Self Portrait: German Bight
    Just before Solstice: Cromarty
    The Firth in Winter
    Days West: Tyne
    Forecast: Thames
    Dover Beach
    Navigator: Fitzroy
    Lundy Notebook
    Writing Home: Irish Sea 1
    A Pint of Dark: Irish Sea 2
    Women in Malin
    Scalpay
    Black Houses on Lewis
    Strangers: Hebrides
    Light Ships

3. Mexico

The Apple Loft
Counting
Tolling
The Fisherman's Rest:
1. Homework
2. Between Tides
3. The Fisherman's Rest circa 1900
4. Unveiling the Lytham Memorial
5. The Inn Sign
6. The Ash Garden

4. Home Strait

Home Strait
Inland
Return to Curlews
Peninsula
Adagio
Grave Goods
Schedule of Dues
Learning Whimbrel
Inheritors
Drawn
A Herring Feather
Carravagio at Emmaus
Writing the Late Self Portrait
Inventory
Meeting John Heath Stubbs
Briggflatts
Tenebrae

Notes and Acknowledgements

1. Outlook

Outlook

Whole seascape in west window; parallels
of islands, turf knolls where thrift aerials tremble;
eel weave of channels where three rivers blend
fresh and salt water, as distillery.

Inside calmed fisherman's cottage driftwood shelving
exhibits sea shells, bottled fleet line astern,
glass case of knots. Barometer's falling weather
is fingering dial, as backing Change to Storm.

Tenants bring sets of lenses, one for close
reading, field glasses for coast's middle distance,
to track from call pied piping oyster catcher,
gowned heron poised to spear the shallows' mirrors,

its stick and feather kit, its angled listening
waiting, as woman thoughtful in observance.
She turns to ask about a change of weather,
waves gnawing at the bays, and marram ramparts.

Bird book and maps all necessary library,
a hammock sag of pages, Latin names,
red letter sketch maps outlining habitats,
as ice retreats, as oceans drown the islands.

Third person's third eye steadied by splay of tripod,
focuses silver veins where tide's declined
as taking photographs of all that's lost;
hears warning trembling in a curlew's echo.

Middle Sea View

Pencil line horizon halves the window,
furred by salt showers, that frames sea air and water,
the changing blues of islands through the evening.

He works in water colours, watching weather
arrive and pause, fill sails and nets of squalls,
lean to the wind like yawls with full rigged clouds.

The cottage walls, a harbour of shipping pictures,
are papered in sea lights, blues, edge of greys.
Everything's stacked and stored, tight as a cabin,
beach combings lodged among the driftwood shelves:
a frayed knot, rusting tin, brine prickled glass,
starfish, marled feathers, gull's skull, small change of shells.

The stairs rise taut as rigging towards the patch
of sky in skylight, past the mahogany frames
sheltering the West Coast paddle steamer fleet.
Decks bulge with Clyde day trippers. With angled smoke
boats turn to islands out of crinolined wakes,
prompt to timetables mounted on matt black

for Oban, Mull, Staffa, Outer Hebrides,
Kyle of Lochalsh, Mallaig, the Clyde Coast, Skye.
They sing the names announcing Spring in childhood:
Hunter's Quay, Kirn, Dunoon, Kilgregan Cove,
Clock Point... Then wartime boom of sword edged prows,
Clyde Atlas veined with yards, then empty spaces

peering south out of Renfrew, Cowal, Dumbarton
to the Cock of Arran, the island's Gaelic crags;
the last page opening blank onto Atlantic.

He works against grained weather, drums his fingers
to beats of rain that bar the Kilbrannan Sound;
his easel, angled; table set for light.

The Weather Door

Behind the door the shed retains some summer,
afternoon warm, right place to reach for green,
the tinned sheen that repels drift of wet weather;
a brush somewhere among cracked pots, and trowels.

Season of maintenance, so appropriate costume
of oldest duffel coat, its dangling rigging,
worn acorn shine of toggles just hanging on,
splashed with preservative from earlier workings.

Stubble jaws on the timber overlap
deepen to an evening green as news becomes
memory: the whimbrel's bill a curve of strand,
the crofter's attic, thatched with a sky of skylight.

Balding, stubbed brush works oiled skim into woodwork,
to face down winter when the weather closes.
Hasps squealed, click fastened with a beak of lock:
west backing south west: Good, becoming Fair.

Weather Maps

One pupil asked: 'Sir, where does weather come from?'
The postman brought the answer in brown wrapping,
unstamped but sent out on Her Majesty's Service,
overnight, early hours, whatever the weather.

Each Tuesday, after lunch, was Weather Maps.
Atlantic charts turned classroom to The Met Office
decoding isobars like tree ring contours,
circles of mathematics, tiers of numbers.

Inland they read the wind. The weather vane
signpost astride roof ridge of outdoor classroom;
learned Beaufort Scale off creosoted doors
like rural aftershave, read maximum

and minimum thermometer, with milk at break time,
tin rain gauge funnelling metal dribbled downpour,
barograph with its arm raised in high pressure
to fascist salute. The next lesson was History.

Fieldwork

Low water; exercise along the estuary
of dredge, erosion, fall and eel of steel
drained to show gouge, undercut, and deposit.

From days of teaching geography he imagined
a small group in their wellingtons and blazers
picking their way from tracks across salt tussocks

to gather and peer down. See how strong tides
have joined the river to burrow and undermine,
sketch out the course, mark out eroded bows

new landforms forming opposite the gap
that winters might cut off; to form A What?
Ox bow lake, sir. Make a note of it.

That wider picture on the minutes back;
story about the ford the Romans made,
the small church nestling in a preaching space

for nearly a thousand years, the carved out cross
found chiselled into lintel when the porch
was added to shield south door from driving rain.

Learning: ways wintering geese within the weather,
pink feet or barnacle, a guide would answer
turn towards Spring across incoming water.

Signs

He went outside to read The Weather Forecast,
comparing notes with breeze that riffed the trees
with sawn off pressure systems in The Atlantic,
even as spots of rain blotted his news.

He kept watch to decode the signs and symbols,
trail of a cold front like an egret's crest,
wind signalled in a drift of convict arrows,
snow drawn as starlight; out of focus fog.

Obituaries, legacies of sun and rainfall
from Aberdeen to Swansea, then Tiree,
and prophecy setting out The Five Day Forecast,
slight Spring breeze rippling pages of his newsprint.

He took the paper as kneeler for his weeding,
clearing dead leaves to let the snowdrops drift,
ground still chilled in the frost shrouding that garden,
cold where he lingered; cloud shadowing her name.

Closing to Home

Liturgy: draft, psalm, anthem; incantation,
a map of water adrift without foundation,
defined by rigid lines, network on ocean,
Lundy and Fastnet.

Far end of weather like September sunlight
or someone watching from an upstairs window
each brief wave's forward roll,
North, South Utsire.

No labels or page reference like a text;
nothing antiphonal like the shuttlecock
arching of words across carved choir stalls,
Malin and Hebrides.

And not all bordered with a landing place.
Some, Bailey, Forties adrift in only ocean.
Radio complements the weather glass,
Cromarty, Forth, Tyne.

Out late, you pick it up, closing to home
down known roads with the backwash of the lane,
and wake of parting hedges, sharing weather
with Fair Isle, Viking.

Night Stair

What we remembered most within the abbey
was the Night Stair leading down like Jacob's ladder
from slept cells as cowled monks filed to their stalls,
steps hollowed out by centuries of sandals.

Candles shivering in draughts, words so familiar
they could say them in their sleep, and may have done so,
like radio leading landward; Rockall, Malin,
like a woman's late Amen at stroke of midnight.

Psalms altered day by day like Beaufort's Wind Scale,
metre decoding speed, outlook's effect
like curtains as rain comes in; Good becoming Fair.

Return for next portion of sleep, re tracing steps
as leaving one on watch along night's boundary,
ready to knuckle each oak door at first light.

2. Weather Stations

Chart

Britain's drawn down as chart for weather's outline,
landfall without detail, blank before history's written
as bias and record on geography's design.

Forms diagram round a mug, like the earth's curve,
or printed on a tea towel in a landlocked kitchen;
sea areas make a jigsaw as The Shipping Forecast.

Midnight's poetry; salt words, Dover, Wight
squared off to draft some geometry onto water;
Hebrides, memories of how the deer were cast
across an island's cooling bars of evening.

Same mountain profile as the barograph
traces the lope of gales and settled weather,
the seal haul spotted off the peninsula,

as we might ask the way to Rockall, Malin,
as capturing coastline framed in ink and wash,
edges, where land dissolves, where line is coastal,

tideline antiphonal as liturgy:
Plymouth, Sole, Fastnet, Lundy; Irish Sea.

Taking Reference: South East Iceland

About imagining somewhere you have not been
by borrowing memories from elsewhere in that country
hardly encountered, South East Iceland, yet

taking reference. Moon landscape after landing,
the outdoors indoors in the hotel paintings,
that Northern Light design of the cathedral,

and photographs: that child as spirit of steam
watching the geyser, that glacier from the air,
arteries of ice. Nipped day: quick slip to dark.

And in the light of slides, close ups of moss,
oranges, crimsons among frond limes, chrome green,
and finding them again on Cumbrian fells,

small moats round boots when walking towards the skyline,
same crouch among those worn shoulders of granite,
that watercolour of similar mound of moorland,

twanged local names reminding of the Icelandic.
Norsemen at landfall would have known that home
as recognition on their first arrival.

Wearing Viking

Another squall, as Norsemen's visit and warning,
stings Hamnavoe, legacy of Viking word hoard:
loan words for writing, also poet's shelter, shieling.

I board with extra cargo, leaving Orkney
with recent purchase from the charity shop
bought opposite his flat, a grey blue gansey
baggy as shower cloud. I half expect his name,

George Mackay Brown, to grace the collar bone,
a fray of cuff betray his writing hand
from when he's conjured Magnus, saint and martyr,
in fountain pen, on sheets of Basildon Bond.

Sail south, past sentinelled Old Man of Hoy,
arguably sea road tracked by founding fathers
voyaging from Viking, Fair Isle, down through Malin
to use Man as a doorstep into England.

Lancashire coast, first, eventual Cumberland;
I'll write the continuing saga, wearing Viking,
sail grateful into futures loaned to us.

Vote of Thanks: Fair Isle

Not Sydney or Grand Canyon but those islands
gathered near Shetland, penned on charts as Fair Isle,
as bucket list or travellers' tale. Imagine
gales' belfries in the green roll of a sea swell.

Picture it second hand from a film's memory,
talk to some who have been there. About trees
layered to bushes by honed blades in the wind.
Gather the odd story from patched conversations;

like the island of a few families who never spoke,
kept separate by a wafer page of doctrine
a Calvinist would struggle to adjudicate;
disputed reference stranded by the Reformation.

Then Sixties people came, stitching a living
from some digging, here, or re-siting a shed,
over there, or helping with some basic care
for a woman's father, no longer fit to croft.

That last time not a lot was said, as usual,
but just before they left some tea was served,
and by each cup a boiled sweet was placed
as quiet ceremonial, vote of thanks.

Exile: Forties

Open the black book; its first story
tells how the world was conjured by a god
spelling out creation. Since then theologians

have been at work, some eager to ask:
Who set the several days as poem,
as answer to darkness, and its crying out?

Perhaps an exile might have once imagined,
to re-establish history and foundation,
such parable of how the world was grounded.

In the beginning... Nothingness of ocean,
abstract of emptiness, then sudden beam,
and opening to the silvering of an evening.

Long before lines and labels on The Shipping Forecast
that white wing, when whole universe was water,
sent out to seek a beach or landing harbour.

Blank space of Forties. First cry of albatross
defining through its measuring rod of wing span,
taking a sounding coded as the Book of Genesis.

Now sea's arranged and named with boundary markers,
like days between old darkness and new stars,
Prisoners in moonlight: *Tell it us again.*

Late Self portrait: German Bight

Their common language, water, fresh and salt,
translating into mingling, English, Dutch,
where German Bight logs Dogger, holds its tongue.

Far side of the Shipping Forecast; the beckoning finger
of Holland introduces Rembrandt's country
seen from the air like polder glimpsed from flight path.

His view still ours whenever a militia jostles
into a night watch, wherever an account of terror
lightnings a ruler's face like a king's vision.

Mostly, as years age, life becomes interior.
Maul stick, his palette, brushes (probably hogs head
crafted by an apprentice) sign such interrogation.

Two planets have risen, circles, on the walls behind him.
He's paused in space, eager in the overlap
as if to beg the question of identity.

His waiting face is graced by slight impatience,
as watching his expression for a change of meaning;
brooding new science as a psychologist.

The study ends after this late self portrait
as setting west, through Dogger, Humber, Tyne,
as evening tide drains oils from the light.

Just before Solstice: Cromarty

End of the roads; the single decker bus
decants last passengers from Inverness.
They pause, unmoored, to trim to the measure of the wind.

Weather exhales full sail, riggings of washing
snap, strain, threatening to tow the wynds and cottages
east, down the Firth, out into Forties, Fisher.

Edgeland from inland, below hunched shoulders of Sutors,
the village is set square, coastline right angled
as Victorian hinge, clamping it to hinterland.

Tidal fields roll away to sky like imports
from somewhere in England, ironed out like that accent.
Not really highland or island, though argument

about ground's founding, and the origin of the world
was drafted here, set scripture against geology,
Hugh Miller layering time through old red sandstone.

Today his cottage, narrow as an indrawn breath,
is part of the tourist trail as tartan wrappings,
a shopping list brief amble from the coach park:

antique emporium's bowl of cricket balls;
craft jewellers, where salt light is cast in silver;
a flyer for string quartets, film's festival

that celebrates dark matinee of the year,
opening with drams around a flapping brazier:
first sequence shown outdoors, draped round the lighthouse.

Quiet in mid morning dawn, just before solstice,
but coming out of the distance on a westerly,
from flayed land of boned granite, a plaid haunting.

The Firth in Winter

Knife point in grey shale; slit, twist, prise, old strata
opened on shoreline, splayed like mackerel gutting;
cross-section of a fossil fish slabbed to light.

Broken in curve of a plunge, scooped gesture,
jutted bone chin-strap stretched to gulp at ocean,
sheened scales, spread armour's silver overlap,
skeleton fan finnage poised to change direction,
half shields of quivering gills. Barely an eye
returning his stare from that moment of split rock.

He'd thought they might be here, between sandstone cliff
face
and the wide firth, as he chiselled names of the dead,
stonemason turning scientist. He'd sensed time
under his hands, traced rippling strata backwards
to the Genesis orchard. Old divines he'd read
had dated the world precisely counting scriptures,
setting years in stone, knew forty days of rain
covered the firth, let others handle fossils;
believed they must be verdicts drowned in judgement.

He'd traced new lines, hammered open limestone nodules
to find, leaded in the rocks, a spread of shoal;
enough, he noted, to fill a museum table.
He laid this flat fish out on his open hand.

He could turn it over, leave it among quartz cobbles,
red sea-planed sandstone where sea boots slipped on wrack,
where high tide left wedged water for reflection.

Puffed cumulus was greying into early evening,
long, slated wind had chilled his fingers numb
round the drowned fish, its brined bone pattern staining
dark canvas of his dry collectors' bag.

A lightship flashed far out, scything the water.
A warning light. He climbed the coastal path
sensing the dangerous catch in what he carried.

Days West: Tyne

City is defined by river, as ground by water,
as squared stone footings, found a few spade blades down,
define the Roman fort that starts a journey
the width of England; moorland and watershed.

Land rises, falls with backs towards North ocean,
climbing the days west, boot shod walking pace,
city soon stepping back, land wide as sea space,
legions with cotton grass cockades, the curlew

broadcasting through pan handling water music
a fluency that Latin never mastered.
Then evening, breasting skyline, glint of silver
where Solway sparkles, exchanging coast for coast.

Tyne becomes distant rumour over shoulder,
but west coast garrisons will offer shelter.

Forecast: Thames

Think inland; not a sea way but the river
seen over Wordsworth's bridge as moat of power,
to towers and terraces, long parliament;
a fortress barred by laws, set under guard.

An opposite end of scale from field and skyscape
to dominating capital, metallic mind,
financiers' fortress, nothing at human scale;
even the weather mortgaged, up for auction.

Thames rises a long way back as bubble and seep
forms energy of a stream, always ambitious
changing its name as donning gown through Oxford;
dawn kingfisher flash of blues, and rowing crews.

Gravel sizzle of tyres, peddling in to gather
first news, and clip the papers on the early shift;
wintering first towpath light. *Whenn - whenn* of swans
hoisting their cloudbank for the snow that's forecast.

Dover Beach

Dover; November; toilets locked till Easter;
France just a rumour beyond the harbour mark;
tide slopping along the beach, high or low water.

The hotel, stacked white like a wedding cake,
might have been Arnold's vantage point for conflict,
hearing through churn of shingle 'faith's
long withdrawing roar', and classical armies

preparing for a night of battle in their ignorance.
Perhaps something of his grappled force of love
expressed as aftermath of wedding banquet,
turning away soon after to draft his stanzas?

Classics are barely taught. A few custodians
quote them in obscure corners of college rooms,
and churches empty like the withdrawing tide;
yet somehow love goes on, in some translations.

Navigator: Fitzroy

Recalling, like those days of gathering evidence,
when storage space for latest specimens
was tight as air before thunder erupted,

assessment of collection; a rubbery squeezing
of octopii in glass jars blown for one,
an altered naming in indelible ink

as Finnisterre to Fitzroy in his honour.
He'd guided The Beagle down the very edge
of Genesis, found how first days of creation

were being re written through the finches bound
to punctuate their change from coast to coast.
He'd open the dictated text, and find it changed.

Torturers had come aboard, hooded accusers,
who circled him in dreams with accusations
he'd undermined foundations of Creation

by piloting a blasphemer, and his theories.
(Some said that Darwin drafted in 'Creator'
as afterthought, to grace his wife's piety.)

Yet west of France, as catching the lift of freedom
in salt swell through Atlantic, Fitzroy's named
as navigator, though dying by his guiding hand.

Lundy Notebook

Ship's master Denver Scions (good Devon name)
noted with crew, deck hands, chief engineer;
roll call for voyage out before first light,
nudging west into Atlantic, bound for Lundy.

Several leagues after darkness, silver spreads
to plate calm waters. Mixture of longhand, shorthand
records noon's landfall (gritty grey beach, steep cliff track,
bald rock across the plateau, shaft of lighthouse).

Only two guarantees, sailing December
supply ship passengers heard when booking passage:
one, that you might not get; two, not get back.
But now a storm's fled east: barometer's fair.

Jottings: the vicar over for a monthly visit,
(any day Sunday when he takes a service).
The agent's census (residents twenty eight),
his whisky. Mugs of tea with lighthouse keepers.

Evening brought early trawl of constellations,
a fresh page (never before so many stars).
Earlier the island gathered for a couple, leaving;
brief headline in long chronicle of smugglers, pirates.

(Names: nature warden, farmer, child's pet goat),
and turning spiral pages re-discover
story of Victorian priest, the Reverend Heaven,
his grave among gold glories of his kingdom.

Writing Home: Irish Sea 1

Grew up within sea's hearing, in new housing
labelled a post war Drive; a sandy track
hinted of origins, slight rise to dyke,
and marsh blotted with hollows gouged from saltings.

Not so much coast as argument of water and ground
where open sea was funnelled to an estuary.
Almost Dutch history: marsh drained, town built on sand.
We looked west; ships pegged out along the horizon.

First memory metronome as shankers' carts
were clopped to shrimping grounds by patient horses
following the tide's pull, lantern route over darkness.
Pause as that poise to follow out low water.

Nearer, a garden with its wound of poppies,
its stretch out down to a field with cropping ponies;
all the room in the world for a child to grow
before the confining move to the town's webbed street map.

Return to the chart: sea areas in their quarterings,
to find where you began, enclosing waters
where Scotland and Ireland seem to reach across
the Irish Sea to mingle each other's language.

Now writing home's ruled blue again; horizon,
old sea still there, miles North of first discovery.
Woods fall away, and from the fell the prospect
fills all the bottom of the sky, and grants continuance.

A Pint of Dark: Irish Sea 2

Each evening, as venturing out under cover of darkness,
night crossings spanned the seaways out of Mersey
to literary Dublin, troubled Belfast town,
each wake decoding parting of the ways.

First visit was North, just before bombs and bullets
divided lives, yet notably Protestant town
kept subject by its castle, and dark gospel.

Much later, meeting a priest along the border,
waiting his lateness as the light declined.
Eventual tea: 'I see you made good time.'

Then, wary country. That evening a city bistro,
red and white gingham cloths, a stroganaff;
wondering if winter was the shooting season.

And, looking back, also in Yeats's city,
a copy of Heaney in tweed jacket pocket;
an overnight up a creaking Trinity staircase.

Reporting back as tourist; notebook, passport
lunch time lasagne reading The Irish Times,
and overhearing some talk about Flann O'Brien,

and realising how long it would take to know
that other country, beyond the Guinness and bookshops,
as sipping that pint of dark to toast arrival,

as reaching out to a round of Dubliners,
not only Joyce's dead committed to memory
but also the fiddler busking in Grafton Street,
and marchers in downpour honouring the hunger striker.

Women in Malin

Subject and object; plaid woman in a photograph
taken just before leaving. The exodus
ordered as the island foundered without a people.
The other making a home in the twenty-first century,
coming with her camera to renovate a croft;
song on the wind, collie at her right hand.

First stilled in sepia, stood with her back to the past,
small field behind her: all I have ever known.
Lines on her face a diagram of runrig
her father raised, she planted as his legacy.
She stands quiet, her face beyond reaction,
paused to gauge next squall out of Atlantic.

The other answers her history, traces her name
from a book a stranger wrote about the island.
Now she takes evidence; the sickled bay,
reeds doubled in the loch, the one road home
as propped against streaming sky in ladder shudder.
She watches the west for a bridging loan of brightness.

So little about them. One without a name
a mother might summon to set a crack of sheets
on a line tautened by breeze. The other
pictured on a strand, her camera's tripod legs
braced for catching dusk through its sieve of light,
her Gaelic knowing each first name among these islands.

Scalpay

You could sit out here all day; nothing would happen.
A tide might stain the slipway in the lochan,
gulls would glide over, trailing cries and shadows,
hard plait of gneiss and turf folds darken, lighten,
small waters smooth, then pattern to a salmon skin.

Sky would be kneaded, rise to spread a squall
creating a widening stipple on open water,
and blot the painter's sheet or punctuate
a line before it's written, glaze a new stone
as it's lifted for setting, matt the colour scheme
of lichen along brown runnels of a worn tin roof.

You could look at the rock and count four billion years,
read of a range of mountains higher than
Andes or Himalaya, see these hills
worn low by this same rain, sense how it was
changed gradually each day; how it goes on.

Black Houses on Lewis

Black from peat smoke in the room, tar on the keel,
grain in the stone, night in the winter hymn,
hours in prevailing dark, or mooring of house
end on to west wind.

A bending low to enter, or look in;
every doorway narrow as a sermon's judgement.
Plaited ropes hold the thatch, draped on wigged roofs
with dangling boulders.

They are set in time like the giddy standing stone,
once a cathedral, rearing down an offside lane;
once signpost and gathering ground, now afterthought's
mystery in peat smoke.

Present tense broadcasts crofts against stretched skies,
sparse seeding of level land where wild air thrums
like a fiddle string tightened for a Gaelic song
of ocean beyond headland.

Last stop before true North: siege engine ocean
pummels and shatters, each surge a disputation
up vulnerable crevice and runnel. The lighthouse stands
scything its beam.

Given the right cast of light, St Kilda enters
fifty miles out, its village a shades' shieling
set out like a story lodged in stone weight black book
each house would shelter.

Strangers: Hebrides

Across the width of desk a weave of tweed,
same pattern as tractor tyres' draft on machair;
shades interlock. Blue greys, as evening deepens.

Strangers, our route's defined by maps with numbers
counting out standing stones, and studios
pacing Atlantic's compass needle road

red as a vein against a potter's palette.
He dips in slip from lowering sky, or turf line
from moor, after peat cutting; rimmed white strand.

His cups, and plates all part of his gallery market
sited down side track, guided by wear of ocean;
bright yolk of oilskin in a lambing painting,
backwash of tidal light in water colours.

The cards make passports for a returning journey
to rented croft's steep staircase to the skylight,
with rocking chair still there, the room to write

where view is mainly sky, small window angled
also to ground held place by boulder boundaries,
a lochan landscape founded out of water.

Nearest track snakes a mown path through the garden,
past willow hedge, and autumn weighted rowan,
to pause at shoreline where the seal might enter.

Light Ships

Five lights guide darkness from this midnight room,
two of them named, the inn, and a friend's home.
Perhaps she is painting, still recalling sunlight.
A third marks halfway house from dale to coastline.

Last two spell endings; somewhere where trickling dunes
hold out as slant and rampart against high waters:
grey, reaching waves tumbling with unfurling surf,
gnawing at England, planing shore, shifting boulders.

Lightships might pitch and clang in similar darkness,
named on a chart among anonymous seaways,
Mersey Bar, Blackwater, beckoning to a safe passage,
a blink against mid winter's brimming solstice.

Watch from this study window; nothing moves.
There is no sound from stars, west wind has fallen,
long rain paused. One. The usual woods and fields
are draped in crepe like shared space among mourners.

3. Mexico

Mexico was a barque, wrecked off Southport, Lancashire on 9 December 1886. She was repaired only to be lost in Scottish waters in 1890.

The Apple Loft

John made it possible, wedging the steps
against the wardrobe, climbing first to lift
the trap door, raising its arc to lock,
calling, guiding my footsteps through the gap.

That loft held a whole autumn. Each spaced fruit
eclipsed its shade on a carpet of used news.
Sunlight poured over skylight, sealed their smell,
tartness of Howgate Wonders, blushed George Caves.

The chest was stowed under a slant of beams.
It promised treasure; as we eased each hasp
its lid protested, fell back, chimed the wall.
We started to search the postcards for survivors.

They had kept their sepia, bearded lifeboatmen,
unsmiling, knowing their duty, uniform
in sou'westers, pregnant in lashed cork supports.
I imagined them answering flares, beginning to row.

That, then, was all I knew, and that pennies from the sales
were given to families weeping behind closed doors
in borrowed black, darning nets for other crews.
I came down out of the sky; left apples, ripening.

Counting

Shouts after the flares! A child counted:
'One, two'; a race to grab sou'westers,
to secure a place in the lifeboat, a sovereign
rode on an oar in that lean shrimping season.

The coxswain nodded them in: 'fourteen, fifteen',
too many for the boat, 'a bit of bother'
over the places. 'Double man some oars,
you'll need the strength.' The west screamed.

They harnessed up the team, five, six, began
a strong plod south, parallel to the sea, three,
four, iron rimmed miles. They launched 'Eliza Fernley'
onto a lashed sea. Full tide. Pummelling breakers.

The boat pitched, reared, rode surf. Rain, hail
came in, pellets in the eyes, agonies in arms,
salt on lips. The boat veered, plunged,
sky became deafening sea, stars blackened.

Muscles threatened to tear, oars to snap,
a gap, the Bog Nut, channel to the 'Mexico',
barque on the land side, riding without lights;
no life, a torch smoking like a fading cry.

Trunk Hill Brow, a sounding, seventeen, eighteen;
an anchor ready for throwing, a green sea, rising,
cartwheel falling, iced wing, whole world turning.
The boat lolled, belly blown, keel to the clouds.

Men swept aside grabbed at frayed lines
draped like seaweed in this flooded dark.
One man lunged, grabbed legs, a thwart;
pressed his mouth to a valve, and kept it pressed.

Each trough plunged them again to drowning depth,
then air would swell in under shuddering gunwales.
Shouts: a register in that sodden darkness,
fresh counting of survivors, plea for lights.

Night inside out, black swell, flood, bodies,
tide on the ebb, John Jackson trying to stretch
frozen legs, tread out cramp, touched bottom,
paced again found sand, eight feet, six . . .

Henry Robinson ducked under a gunwale, said:
'I thought there were nine men under the boat
at first, three left when I went away.
I do not know what became of the nine'.

These two waded through ebb shallows, walked home
with the wind from the sea also awash in trees.
One knocked on a neighbour's door, then two
'To see if they had come home. They had not'.

Night watch: the low hours, one, two. At three
a sighting. Drowned boat. Three beneath her.
Another on the shore. 'He expired soon after.'
One knee deep in water. 'He died in hospital.'

Some were coiled in webs of oars and lines.
Other bodies were found in various positions
on the beach. Counting. Fourteen men lost.
'Most of the Southport fishermen could not swim.'

Tolling

The town bowed, summoned by the mourning belfry,
where ringers toiled four hours through the Mexico funerals,
pulling and pausing on ropes as sailing sound.

Brass bands played The Mariners' Hymn:
'For those in peril on the sea'. In hail, sleet
the crew was mustered in coffins. A fleet of closed carriages
took the pale mourners, shivering with grief.

Seventy minutes for the procession to pass
each frozen spot. Hymns. A sermon. Hard rain
deepening the best shades of the Sabbath black.
Planks oozed; ropes dripped on the new brick vault.

Eleven days to Christmas, and low tide of light,
night stalking early on the estuary,
across the marshes, inlets and shrimping grounds,
North Hollow, Granny's Bay; those other funerals

of the St Anne's crew, thirteen lost. Tolling:
twenty seven drowned, sixteen widows.
Fifty orphaned. Counting: twelve saved.

The Fisherman's Rest

1. Homework.

Someone had done their history homework, gathered
pictures in this pub, now called The Fishermen's Rest,
left when the hotel covering several acres
came down. A smug estate was built on sand.

Inside, above the clicks of pool players' shots,
gale rages through the strained hemp of the barque's
keeling storm rigging. Above flock chairs, a blackboard
on mock Victorian wallpaper boasts of Steaks.

In *The Fairground Nineteen Fifteen,* women stroll
in ankle length dresses, through wartime; keep their distance.

2. Between Tides

Not knowing where to put their land locked bodies
fishermen lean on railings, kippering.
They are heavy in salted seaboots, hands in pockets,
doldrummed in jerseys knitted for the gutting winds.

Not knowing where to look between summer tides,
they hang around, like beached crabs at low water;
wait for the freshening breeze, shift of a keel
tug at the moorings, gathering of tackle.

Wait for the list to the banks and bloom of nets,
adequate catch, a night wind to safe harbour.

3. Fishermen's Rest Circa 1900

Exposed brick walls, rough mortar, a planked door,
two small ships scratched into the drifts of splinters:
chalked fishing boat, drawn swollen with full sails;
oared lifeboat, gear stowed, stripped down to storm warning.

Three boatmen sit, more than a century ago;
warmed backs to the wall, measuring the state of light,
trim of the cloudbanks, gauging the stage of the tide,
weighing risks in empty hands, storm against catch.

Leave here on any night with a south west gale:
same salt in the rain, a boomed wind's requiem

4. Unveiling the Lytham Memorial

A top hat shimmers like a liner's funnel,
winks code like a signal lamp. The modest bowlers
stand like a blackened road of close packed cobbles;
Sabbath best bonnets turn, a ribbon flutters.

Aisles widen through the crowd, taut children crisp
in junior bowlers, boaters, sailor hats,
line the route to the statue's lashed sou'wester.
Carvings peers out from crags the height of masts.

Dignitaries process to unveiling, a ripple,
so distant from storms, through dipping, policemen's helmets.

5. The Inn Sign

Two anglers sit with rods among the reeds;
one flaunts a flapped deerstalker, sports plus fours,
cultivates a moustache, fiddles with his bait box,
lets his line idle from a tilting cane.

His friend squats on a creel, watching the water
with indifference that a languid summer brings.
Trees stand still on the inn sign: 'The Fishermen's Rest',
misunderstanding the name, the morgue where brine

dripped from sagged bodies lifted from sodden sands,
brought to this nearest shelter with struggling lanterns.

6. The Ash Garden.

You lie three miles from the sea;
stilled, in a harbour of trees
whose names the leaves recite
through sycamores, oaks and birches.

You were brought to summer resting
on a warm day without wind,
a place of grass and birdsong.

Gardeners prepared your ground,
a cube cut out of land
where sea sand turned to peat,

and the town flowed out to farmland.
Few words, a small urn, tilting,
firm tread on the square turf lid,

a pause; a drifting away.
We left flowers bright in sunlight,
we met the next, slow hearse.

You lie three miles from the sea;
you can hear the tide as wind
plunges inland during gales
through sycamores, oaks and birches.

4. Home Strait

Home Strait

High water; bluebells chime, and flood the wood.
The walk back starts by wading through their colour,
their purple inking oak, and hazel shadow.

Home strait: just tracks the three miles from the church,
almost all woodland. Eight boot steps cross one road;
risings and fallings like a weather forecast.

Wind in a beech wood gives its way to water,
the river urgent under stone rainbow arch.
Pillars and back-lit leaves form altar window,

and turn a wide hollow of copse into cathedral.
Rare space across slant field marks Herdwick pasture;
the turn west backs against cloud rifling fells.

Stick's braced against steep scree of riddled gravel;
a cuckoo echoes, pheasants cough, mid-morning cockerel
sends its haloo across a brace of farms.

Two streams; then open ground where larch was felled
coming back into its own as rippling birch,
lamp lighting gorse. Cream layers among the rowan

balance like plates along a waiter's arm.
Stick tap has guided another along these hill tracks,
his boots and similar tweed part of walk's ceremony.

Top a rain gutted rise, and sea's still there
like separate sky on woodland across five fields.
Beyond immediate thorn a tumbling cloudbank

sent inland out of Man forecasts changed weather.
Now downhill all the way to cottage harboured
in rinse of bluebells drafted in blue black shade

as close confining, and a reaching out,
essay and exercise; same dark line ruling
we always find when walking towards the coastline.

Inland

Moors become ocean as we venture inland,
a thousand feet above sea level, and yet
same vastness, and similar crucible of weathers;
distances ebbing and flowing as skies dissolve.

Not so much driving as navigation, a weave
along more hospitable contours, past stone farms
that even in early summer's gathering light
crouch down out of the wind, braced against gale force.

Most bird call is invisible; somewhere beyond
a fluttering beech wood curlew reminds of coastland;
lapwings dismantle flight as shifting ladders;
a gull, blown landward, skis above fugitive deer.

Back on familiar ground, the lizard ridges
of fells whose names we know cool after molten
light leaves the North sky late this time of year.
Along the coast we've learned waves stretch as tide turns.

Return to Curlews

Late roses turn the church memorial garden
flesh pink against named granite's evening grey;
list with its back to weather within this wrong
season. No curlews on autumn's Saxon fields.
Sea wind has harried harvest, and the ash trees
are turned back into skeletal frames of peacocks.

Scanning these names turns memory to remembrance;
sometimes a full life, sometimes just nod, regret
returning as all we offer, from far off;
our own times as that evening when the choice
was staying, reading, or following familiar route
along the lonning like a ramp to sky's light.

Walk followed earlier century, hardly a car
passes that way: slim tarmac nibbled by winters,
its central grass stripe curved green like punk's haircut,
its rise to limestone outcropped like Roman outpost.
Closer to hand hay meadows, wind winnowing sedge,
becks' overflow, peat mottle of the gathering flock,

as curlew after curlew stretched that evening,
their calls made echo in the faltering waver
played across landscape; climbing ropes strung silver.
Never before such aerial rivulet,
high claim and mapping of land as nesting sites.
Never again such promise in the curlews' music?

Peninsula

Those final miles all water instead of ground,
crossing the sound; thumped heartbeat of the steady ferry;
details of bay and field re-form the mainland.
Clanged metal jaw grates slipway like a drawbridge.

Road follows coastline. There is no other way
edging through anticline where a heather cross
flares in appropriate purple. Cattle grid rattles
a snare drum warning, both entrance and returning.

Going back means lifting a latch on a borrowed croft,
and re-establishing ritual at the ruined chapel
where oxen are carved on a stone as a ploughing team,
their owner known without a register.

You imagine medieval monks who turned this ground,
psalm by psalm, into a benediction.
You pass through their shadowed prayers on entering
through the sandstone rainbow of doorway, turn to see

how light is fading the hill into departure.

Adagio

Downpour re-tunes the burn after a drought
to gargle; strangled song about this plague year.
We hear in our small beck a singing school;
our North's crossed border into first plaid county.

Travel in these locked down limits is imagination
as only way to venture, and return.

Going back conjures the track to the castle gate,
unloosed with a squeal of bolt above low water
setting ruined chapel's silence to tideline's psalter,
evening dress oyster catchers' sole note anthem,

and wide across the Sound carved mountains shadow
an epaulette of gold on a field's shoulder.

Thunder again; as barrels on rubble of cobbles
we heard on that first visit, coming as strangers.
Now each return marks out what's slightly changed
through wear and tear; stacked creels, that abandoned croft

set high to sight coasts lit by sky's late flight
through long adagio of the evening light.

Grave Goods

Inheritance: hundred beads of mouse eyed jet
currency, peppercorn black among flint scrapers,
barbed and ridged arrowheads, an arc of urn,
shell of food vessel; provisions for the journey.

Honours and mourning as they set his course
in barrow shape, an upturned boat's stone cargo
pointing over fellscape to late Northern light,
poised as slack water through those long June evenings.

Boulder boned arthritic spine, a question mark,
why barrow was paid out during excavation's
real time some sixty years ago; four thousand
summers of tidal bracken since the internment.

Now just the most apparent shadow among
suspected thirty graves across the cairn field,
picked out elastic shadows at low tide of light
that catches billow of mound, stubbed clue of kerbstone.

No body; never a question of resurrection,
not simplest hint of outline on a shroud.
Most cairns remain untapped in rippled ocean
of sedge, spiking long views to racks of mountains.

One day the archaeologists might return
with their own grave goods to find what hunters gathered,
their fine point trowels unearthing a forensic season
to scrape back time; cross question brief evidence.

Schedule of Dues

None come now with sprat barrels and hampers of rabbits
to pay their dues for passage on the island ferry
in the old bills, by cartload; counting-house shillings and pence.

Nobody now fingers their sporrans for fourpence
to ship rolls of fencing wire; counts out one and sixpence
for a cow, bullock or bull (aged two years and over),

or tots up coins from threepenny bit small change
to a shining florin, silver as a frosting moon,
for bags, boxes, cartons, parcels and packages,

small barrels, drums, instruments or bags of whelks
coming ashore or wrapping up the island's imports
depending on weight (pigs sixpence, crated or loose).

Top rate was four shillings for wedders, or rams per score;
four times the fare for Passengers to Pier Direct,
and twice the price of a barrel, or two hundred bricks.

Still, a click like a latch is flicked to call the boat over,
turning the white square red on the noticeboard;
a scutter of outboard widening a wake on the inlet.

Today six pounds takes walkers, gripping their poles,
or diners beckoned towards The Boathouse seafood,
or a minister, collared and wide with a vestry of luggage.

Kelped air's stayed, and the shoal of shadow under netting;
plastic red fish box 'Stolen from Coopers, Aberdeen',
lobster pots beached among brambles, a snake charm of
ropes.

None come now with their bags of wool or drain tiles,
when graft was laying clay pipes at a penny a passage,
or ticket grudged coppers for an unaccompanied dog,

or pause for long inside the kirk that Telford
designed for Gaelic psalmody, and lament's
still, softening air, through which the autumn enters.

Learning Whimbrel

He watched the birds by sound after his blindness,
calling to mind from hearing small cassettes,
species from song; each voice, as experts phrased it.

He played tapes in the car, as fingering notes.
Historian, he never saw their geography.
Light was just dawn or dark, denying detail.

Lock on his eyes made prison, but also flight
as birds came, bringing in their ancient music
stories he'd once squint manuscripts to decode.

Tapes brought him gifts of fluency in recognition;
house martins' *trr trr*, or *bier bier* alarms
as harvesters scythed air; adobe nesters.

Locked down by plague, he'd conjure miles they travelled,
tartan migration, by flung songs that he'd heard;
sea eagles' *krick rick* poise, *ge ge* in soar.

His wife would check descriptions in her bird book,
kliep kliep in oystercatchers' black and white;
Lowlanders' *pluit* from an avocet.

Evening in islands, listening from memory,
her hand guided his elbow; his folding cane
probed track for boulder, he caught the lochan's music,

hearing *uid uid uid*, as Nordic phrasing
of whimbrel, mottled plumage like the burn
that flowed among the words she read to him.

Inheritors

Never a father, he sired the inheritors
who follow him along green ways, and the old ways.
He leads them, like Moses, across the wilderness;
Norman Nicholson, poet of pebble and mountain.

He arrived early, sensing in the fiery furnace,
that lit the iron works to an all night sunset,
a smelting of warning. His lines were shod
with need to read a rescue for creation.

His tone, adagio; curlew over estuary,
shadow of Old Man mountain glimpsed from attic.
He transcribed singing stones, of lime and granite,
words his companions, to cast a summoning

to all children through whom flowed veins of ink,
to draft their protests as the weather changes,
following his footsteps where old nature of slag
restores itself in journals of this plague year.

He saw young, like himself, as refugees
from war, as he gasped shadows in the sanatorium;
as flying a box kite into high, blue future,
as he sensed stirred world, breathing within his garret.

He taught them, green grandfather who saw beyond them,
casting his lines as angling for their futures;
calling them from his lock, beyond fells and walls,
to march, design red banners, defy by stanza,

to honour his grace days, and re cast his past
like his sculpted head, clear eyed between hedging sideboards.
That staring into liberation after lock and key;
that miracle, turning a weather vane into a pencil.

Drawn

She begins to draw. From a chair on the other
side of the easel I hear her pencil touch,
held like a torch. She starts to establish outlines.

Her world becomes an oblong of concentration
of A2 heavy cartridge paper clipped
to a sheet of plywood on the angled stand.

Search. She draws me in; subject and object,
collects my face, her pencil changed to pastel
ground from ore at the mine where we are sitting

as in an outdoor studio with the winding gear
set to a shovelled sky. I keep my eye,
as told, set left, watching the middle distance.

She begins to tap and knock as seeking entrance.
Two seconds for each darted glance, a mark;
balancing act between evidence and recording.

She reaches for colour from gear around her feet:
round tins of charcoal, yellow stick, stud of rubber,
a gaping rucksack, tissue, pencil sharpener.

Semaphore. A detail checked, a dab of hand.
I glance to read her face, note her pursed lip.
She is sculpting in two dimensions with her red chalk.

A final flourish; she stands to assess perspective,
tilting her head to read the portrait back.
You would like to ask: 'When do you light the eyes?'

Back home, I set up an easel out of a chair
to return the gaze of this face, larger than life,
hair older, greyed by pencilling on white light

sheening the brow. See how she has moulded cheeks,
recessed the eyes, hoisted the bridge of the nose;
left the mouth tight, as waiting for a leading question.

Portrait: an essay in late afternoon;
its gradual shadow back to a draining light;
a stilled gaze, as acknowledgement of departure.

A Herring Feather

She could have drawn a candle, or the whale's profile
of the whole island, or elastic stretch of breaker.
All morning storm barged in off the Atlantic.

She could have tramped the mile length as a gatherer,
collecting through the shouldering charge of air
studio objects for her still-life class:

dried seaweed clawed arthritic, oystercatcher's
egg blown barren, pebbles with striped years of strata;
bouquet: speared marram, daisy, flared montbresia.

Instead, by light spread through the rattling window,
speckled and salted, cured for watching winter,
she sketched arc, shades and poise of herring gull feather,

not quite finishing but leaving room
to add its cry, streaked lift of gathering weather.

Caravaggio at Emmaus

Ripped elbow draws us in; peek of a sleeve
worn and torn to disclosure of white lining,
tensed as the traveller with half light for a face
finds in a gesture of grace recognisable lightning,

diagonal against the domestic. Thought and gaze
are held, his body a spring of poised amazement,
hand braced intensely on his chair's right arm
as needing a crutched support for revelation.

Moment nudged into eternal; an inn transposed
from Biblical into contemporary. The table's set
without apparent ceremony, a chicken,
with its thorned claws, is ready to be wrenched apart.

Something of earth in detail; those tints of browns
yeasting in well baked loaf, already broken;
leaf's parchment as still growing, ewer's rim,
shadow moating of fruit bowl with its glow of apples,

and slash of late, white light through the chiaroscuro
in starching cloth across the hospitable table.
Landlord left squared off after obedient sabbath;
that pleated prayer shawl casual over Christ's shoulder,

not needing established words to grace his blessing.
Instead, he raises his arm as if expecting
a dove to perch from a flood story or a baptism;
other arm poised to enhance his concentration,

as thinking back to his dark and recent journey,
returning from eternal to this supper gathering;
a still life Caravaggio chose to people,
figures he stilled to life in his crumpled present.

For he was also there; some room for him
in brown space, in the foreground, just beyond
the reach of the older man re enacting a cross
with outstretched arms, gaze lasered on Christ's stigmata.

While standing across from where the artist sketched,
back to thin mist of doubt, theology's shadows,
the innkeeper looks on, one of the supporting cast
history relies on for a dispassionate reading

of how face softens under prayer when bread is blessed,
how hands mould air between pain and its healing,
how shadow seems suddenly stilled on the usual wall.
There is just enough room to draw forward another chair.

Writing the Late Self Portrait

Some days the young woman would find a bench in The Parks
while her husband learned about God in an Oxford college,
and wait until the old woman with her carrier bags
came and lifted some poems from a bulge of papers,
and read to her about Rembrandt, and his savage presence.

Her patient looking, and his looking back.
He mirroring himself in Late Self Portrait.
She copying what she saw into her poetry
from tone and brush stroke, angle of light and shadow.
His gaze across three centuries, almost greeting.

He must have used the same looking glass. She imagined
how he would catch, returning year by year,
those details of decline, dusk softening eyes,
sagged pouchings where you'd stoop to purse a coin,
humanity's costs; its poverty of betrayal.

Hard to work out whatever he was thinking;
student of eyes, that stretch of shadowed skin
below his right cheek hinting at emerging smile
like sunlight opening land on windless mornings,
acknowledging the ache within the nightfall.

Similar costumes: wide way his unbuttoned coat
rose from his heart to frame his questioning,
felt shadow hint of hat, unkempt moustache,
that possible humour under interrogation;
that onlyness of art within the artist.

Same loneliness across the centuries;
an old man taking his brushes to paint the dusk
he was becoming; a woman in her later years
writing of him in the slow fading of the light,
leaving the young woman with time for both of them.

Inventory

He spent life drawing whom he was becoming;
hundred self portraits, signature reflection;
a mirror strapped to easel held his gaze,
meeting his eyes as taking notes, inventory.

Fortune and its collapse led to the listing,
a re-defining judged by what he owned,
identity as possessions; the Insolvency Office
interested to realise goods to pay his debts.

Souvenirs, curios; magpie haul of props:
cuirasses, halberds, coral, gourds, Indian robes,
cast heads of Roman emperors, ranked in history,
busts of philosophers, and a prince's death mask;

'forty seven specimens of land and sea
creatures, and things of that sort', two
terrestrial globes, and an international armoury:
Malayan kris, African spears, assorted pistols;

a dressing room of costumes, and the scallop shell
seen in Christ Healing the Sick, two walking sticks,
assorted stags' horns, helmets, and a lion's skin;
the largest batch of entries sixty art books,

some picturing evaluation – Item Two Hundred:
the precious book of Andrea Mantegna;
some absences that added to his value –
shirts, handkerchieves, twelve napkins at the laundry.

A life signed off: done and inventoried
over two days of strong light in July:
Paintings, Furniture and other Effects in the house
of Rembrandt van Rijn Living in the Breestraat

by the St Anthony Water Gate. And at his death
another listing, later singed by fire,
through Best Room, Vestibule, The Smallest Room:
Twenty two finished and unfinished paintings.

Meeting John Heath Stubbs

Gravy stains on his tie one memory of him,
and seeing him more cautious with his searching cane
in sixties Chelsea than the eighteenth century,

and being steered to a saved space on High Table
where he would angle a menu to remaining light,
squint courses, soup to sweet through plate glass glasses.

I never heard him lecture, but his reputation
surrounded all of us who yearned to write;
how 'Give me a line' could unfurl yards of Pope,

or dared to follow an editor's recommendation:
'You should show him some of your work; I've mentioned you'.
Instead, back to the wall, I watched him pass.

Not a white stick, but more of a magus wand,
as casting spells his next poem would become.

Briggflatts

Sneck clicked again to open this meeting house
that waits for a gathering into collective silence.
An hour might pass without a spoken word;
note only shift of light, overheard birdsong.

Or friends might air concerns brought down the lane
by overhearings from those dangerous protests;
quiet people of first lands, guarding the rain,
met by the powerful with gas and baton rounds.

Shadows. Perhaps the shade of Basil Bunting
who'd cross the country in each summer's light;
pause, to renew his visions for his writing days,
refresh his poetry from Rawthey's madrigal.

Ancient house, gift; outside fells' tapestry
forms backdrop to a bench that hosts Spring sunlight.
We might request from newly planted orchard
a blossom sprig for where the poet lies quiet.

Tenebrae

Slack water; clocks turned back to give more light,
and over the gentle mingle of fresh and salt
flicker and dart as bats bring evening out.

They quarry fluid boundaries, bank and shallow,
as pilgrims, waiting for the ford to settle,
reverence church, altar, cross in the medieval,

trod trackways hard on boots, as to Emmaus
after full light, gathering the stranger's grace.

Bats also close; now blamed from far away
for spreading darkness, fear across a plague year,
wasting in wilderness; the disappeared

like candles, snuffed to dusk, through Tenebrae,
till church is left to dark from Passion's play;
and curlews add their ebb notes to the estuary.

Notes & Acknowledgements

'Learning Whimbrel' won the Norman Nicholson Society 'Lockdown' Poetry Competition in October 2020.

'The Firth in Winter' was awarded second prize in the Keats Shelley Prize, 2007.

'Schedule of Dues' won the inaugural Borderlines, Carlisle Literary Festival Poetry Competition.

Thanks are due to the editors of *The Keats Shelley Review, abridged*, the Norman Nicholson Society 'Lockdown' anthology, *The Unpredicted Spring, Poems* 25, and *Littoral Magazine* where versions of some of these poems were first published.

'Writing the Late Self portrait', and 'Late Self portrait' take references from *Self Portrait by Rembrandt* (late 1650s).

'Inventory' takes reference from Bailey, A., *Rembrandt's House* (New York: Tauris Parke Paperbacks: 2014).

Original quotations in the sequence 'Mexico' are taken from *The Great Lifeboat Disaster of 1886* by J Allan Miller (Sefton Libraries and Arts Services: 1986).

Briggflatts is an historic Quaker meeting house near Sedbergh, Cumbria.

Tenebrae is a church service where the story of Christ's Passion forms seven readings in a candlelit church, in Holy Week, just before Easter. After each reading a candle is extinguished on the altar until the church is left in near darkness. The congregation leaves in silence.

Milton Keynes UK
Ingram Content Group UK Ltd.
UKHW010621101023
430280UK00005B/107